T0085264

STANDARDS
for
Trumpet

VOLUME 1

To access audio visit:
www.halleonard.com/mylibrary

2247-1677-3874-4473

ISBN 978-1-59615-819-1

Music Minus One

EXCLUSIVELY DISTRIBUTED BY

HAL•LEONARD®

7777 W. BLUEMOUND RD. P.O. BOX 13819 MILWAUKEE, WI 53213

Visit Hal Leonard Online at
www.halleonard.com

Bob Zottola

*J*azz trumpeter Bob Zottola played with them all, legends like Benny Goodman, Peggy Lee, Frank Sinatra, Gerry Mulligan, Maynard Ferguson, Chick Corea and dozens of others. With those credits, he could easily rest on his laurels. When Zottola moved to Florida in 2004 after completing a 16-year run in the Broadway orchestra of *Les Miserables*, he was certainly entitled to

a break. He's done anything but slow down. He plays seven nights per week—and a few afternoons as well—and, in the process, is contributing to make Naples a jazz town. Only a world-class player could do that. Becoming world class takes time. Bob Zottola's been at it since childhood, surrounded by music in his native Greenwich, Connecticut home from childhood.

He recalls, "My father, Frank, a trumpet player, was also a violinist and conductor and arranger for the Claude Thornhill big band, right alongside arranger Gil Evans, who would later gain fame for his collaborations with Miles Davis. As a child, my father would take me to Evans' apartment in New York City, and I would play with Gil's dog while my father worked on the orchestrations. There were big band rehearsals at my house constantly, and my father always played records by the great old trumpeters like Bix Beiderbecke and Bunny Berigan. I'm sure I picked up a lot of my musical stuff as a kid by osmosis."

As for the trumpet, his school music director, who knew Zottola's dad was a musician, recruited the youngster for the school band. Zottola ran excitedly home to tell his father, but couldn't decide what instrument to play. His dad pointed at the trumpet resting on top of the upright piano saying, "there it is." It wasn't a love affair between the player and the instrument in the beginning. He wasn't thrilled with the strict, old-world style of teaching, and he describes the sound he heard from his first experiences in a music ensemble

as "horrible." He didn't pick the horn up again until he was 11. It wasn't long after that he began winning prizes and appearing on television and radio. Zottola doesn't use these words, but it's clear he was a child prodigy, touring nationally from the age of 12. "I did television shows like *The Original Amateur Hour, Paul Whiteman's TV Teen Club* and *Arthur Godfrey's Talent Scouts,*" he remembers, "These were talent competitions, and when I won in these shows, the producers would take me around the country, playing for huge audiences with a big band, with orchestrations that were written for me. Eventually, I joined the Godfrey morning show with the pros, and the next thing I know, I was told I had to join the Musician's Union."

This was one successful child performer who seemingly made the transition to adulthood with ease. Support in this area came from an unlikely place: the United States Air Force. "A colonel in the Air Force from Washington, D.C. contacted the band director of my high school. Coincidently, the colonel had been the high school band director at one time. He had heard about me, in that a guy who was leaving the Airmen of Note—the premier jazz big band of the U.S. Air Force—was from my hometown," Zottola recalls. "My dad took me to Washington to audition, and I played with guys like Tommy Newsom, who later found fame on *The Tonight Show*, and Sammy Nestico, who were both in the band at that time. I passed the audition and they shipped me off to basic training. You could make a career of it if you wanted. Sammy Nestico, later to write for Count Basie and many others, was there for 20 or 30 years. I did my straight four years. That seemed like enough; I was itching to get out there and play and do all the things I always dreamed about."

New York City was a thriving oasis in the 1950s, not only as a jazz town, but also as the center for musical work in television, Broadway pit bands, radio and recording studios. An accomplished, studied and versatile player could do very well in the Big Apple back then, and given the many kinds of work available, things were never dull. Zottola's first experience with a name band after military service was with the orchestra of swing era icon Charlie Barnet. Dull it wasn't. "That was less than the romantic dream that I had," he says of the Barnet gig. "I was riding around in Charlie's

car, doing one-nighters." Things improved. As a result of the stellar contacts he made while with the Airmen of Note, the quality of work quickly improved. He was busy in the recording and television studios. Even *The Price Is Right* had a house orchestra in those days. He is particularly proud of his affiliation with "The King of Swing" himself, Benny Goodman. Goodman was asked to put together a big band for the 1964 New York World's Fair. As Zottola describes it, "This was a real all-star band. It was an unlikely group of suspects but it was really terrific. You had players like trombonist Frank Rehak, trumpeter Clark Terry, and just one great player after another."

He had no grand plan for his success in those days, or for today, for that matter. "People ask me how they can break into the music scene," he says. "I didn't go to the drawing board or read a book on business or time management or 'How to Win Friends and Influence People.' If you know what you're doing, people hear you and it just happens. They recommend you to other people. How did I get to play with Benny Goodman? I played with Tommy Newsom for three years in the Airmen of Note. He remembered how I played, so when it came time for him to recommend someone, he recommended me. That's how I got into the studios; I never had an agent. There was no other way other than colleagues recommending you." Having worked next to these giants for so many years, the trumpeter was and is anything but star struck and is anything but a name dropper. When pressed, he mentions his pride in being a part of Frank Sinatra's 'East coast band' of the 1980s, his world tour with Chick Corea in the late 1970s, backing Peggy Lee and playing with Maynard Ferguson's big band.

When *Les Miserables* closed on Broadway in 2003 after 16 years, he had to make some major decisions. "I started doing some substitute work on shows like *Wonderful Town, Chitty Chitty Bang Bang* and *Gypsy*, he says. "But because I had more free time, my wife and I started coming down to Naples more often to vacation. Then the Naples Cafe on Fifth gig started in 2004. It was just a duo gig on a Friday night and I had no idea how it was going to work out. From that it slowly blossomed into Bob Zottola and the Expandable Jazz Band!"

"There's something very, very special about who I call 'The Naples Jazz Lovers.' Part of it might be the nostalgia factor. They lived through the big band era," he says. "They were not exposed to it after the fact. They were there when Benny Goodman gave his Carnegie Hall concert. They were on 52nd Street." Off the bandstand, Zottola is affable, low-key, witty and positive. He takes his music seriously, but not too seriously, and he holds his devoted audiences in high regard. On the bandstand, he's the same way. He lets the music happen, which is how the best jazz is made, and never even suggests how one of his talented sidemen should play. He lets them be themselves and gives each and every one of his players—no matter what the size of the Expandable Jazz Band on a particular evening—ample solo space. This is a rarity. Especially in the jazz business.

- Bruce Klauber, *Naples Daily News*

Visit Bob Zottola at:
naplesjazzlovers.com

MUSIC MINUS ONE

6841

CONTENTS

SOLO B♭ TRUMPET
(FLUGELHORN)

When You're Smiling

Words and Music by
MARK FISHER, JOE GOODWIN and LARRY SHAY

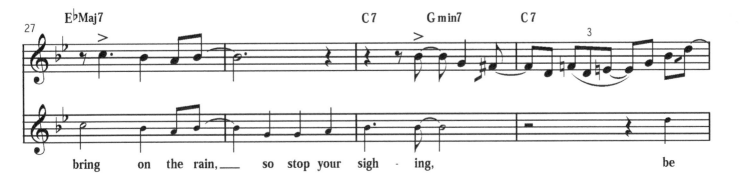

bring on the rain,___ so stop your sigh - ing,   be

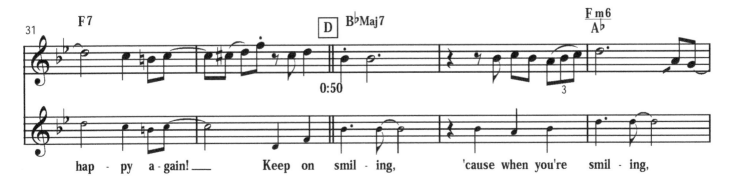

hap - py a - gain! ___ Keep on smil - ing,   'cause when you're smil - ing,

the   whole world   smiles   with   you.

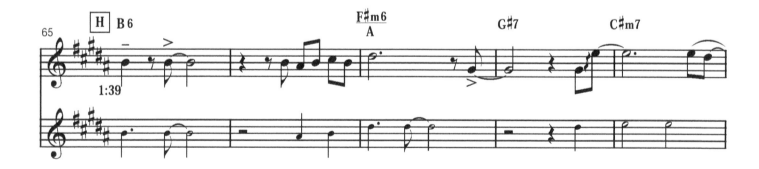

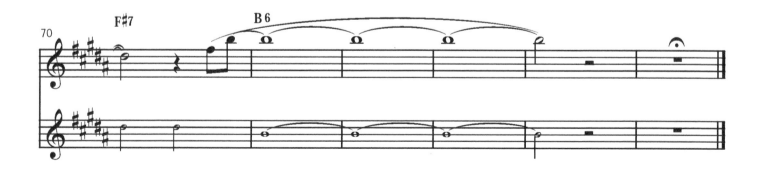

SOLO B♭ TRUMPET
(FLUGELHORN)

I'm in the Mood for Love

Words and Music by
JIMMY McHUGH and DOROTHY FIELDS

MMO 6841

8

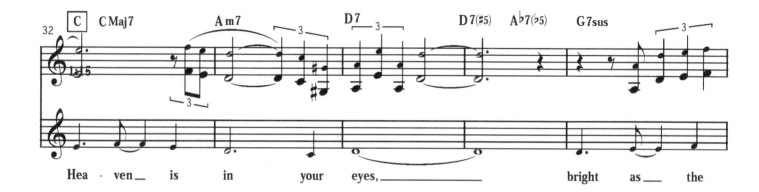

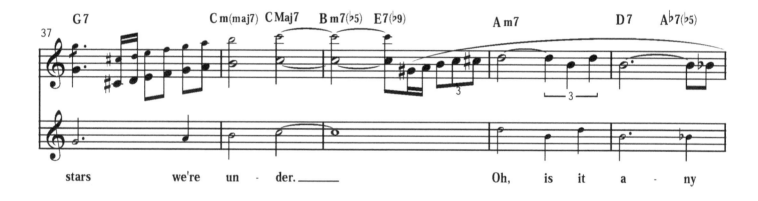

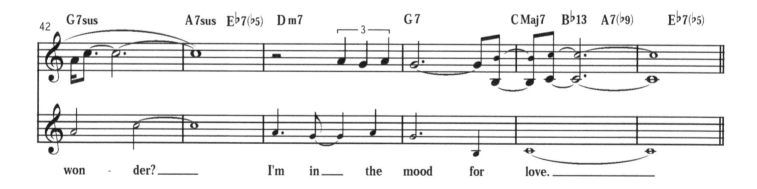

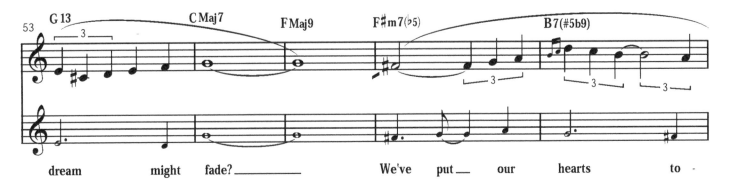

dream might fade? _____ We've put ___ our hearts to -

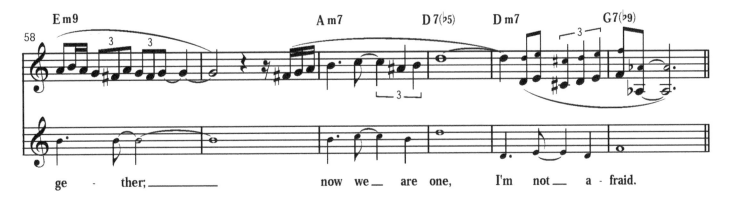

ge - ther; _____ now we ___ are one, I'm not ___ a - fraid.

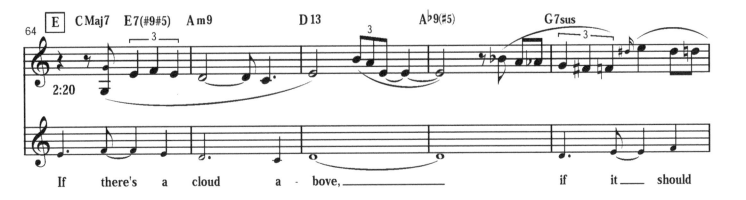

If there's a cloud a - bove, _____ if it ___ should

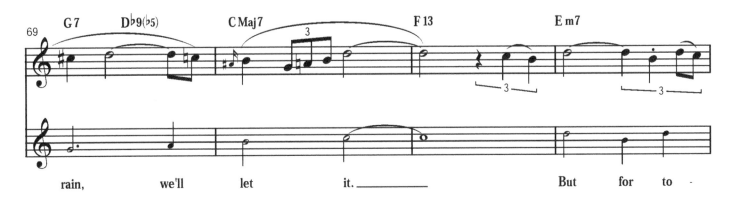

rain, we'll let it. _____ But for to -

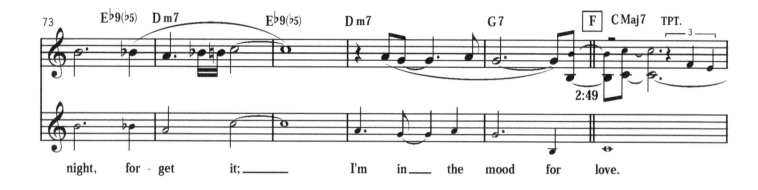

night,   for - get   it;_____   I'm   in __ the   mood   for   love.

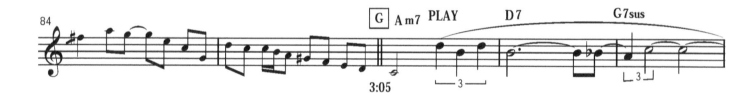

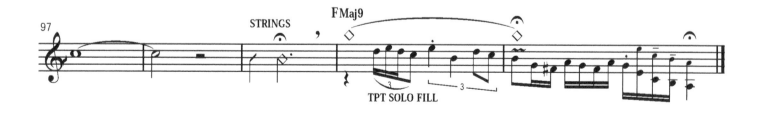

SOLO B♭ TRUMPET
(FLUGELHORN)

Blue Bossa

Music by Kenny Dorham
(Ten/Sop Sx. cues)
BOB'S SOLO

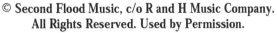

MMO 6841

12

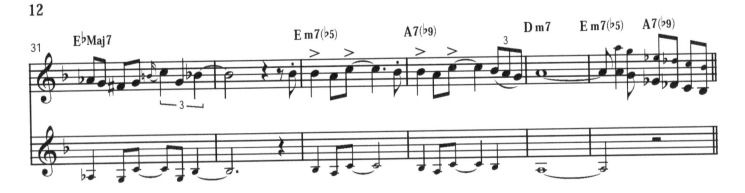

0:53

1:16

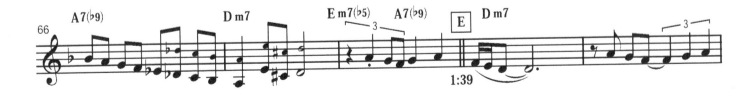

1:39

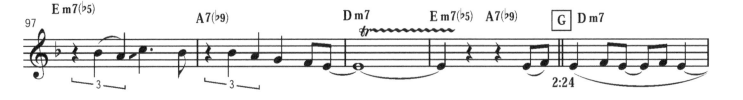

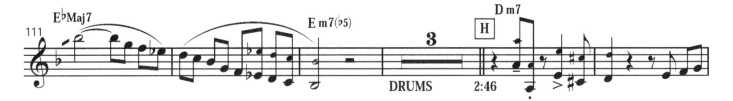

14

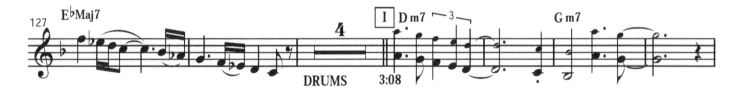

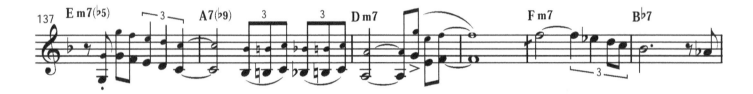

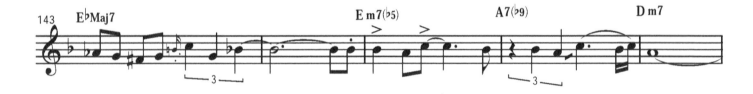

SOLO B♭ TRUMPET
(FLUGELHORN)

How Do You Keep the Music Playing?

Lyrics by ALAN and MARILYN BERGMAN
Music by MICHEL LEGRAND

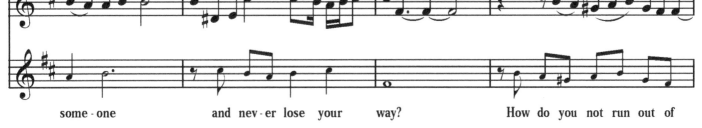

Lyrics under the staves:

How do you keep the mu-sic play - ing? How do you make it last?

How do you keep the song from fad - ing too fast? _____ How do you lose your-self to

some - one and nev - er lose your way? How do you not run out of

MMO 6841

new things to say?_____ And since you know we're al-ways

chang-ing, how can it be the same? And tell me how year af-ter

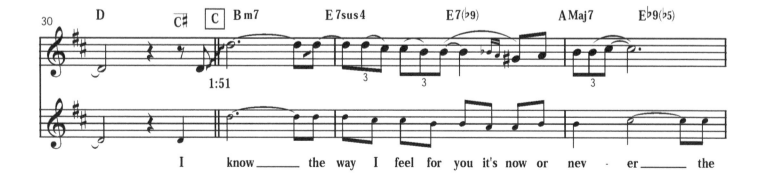

year you're sure your heart will fall a - part___ each time you hear his name?_____

I know_____ the way I feel for you it's now or nev - er_____ the

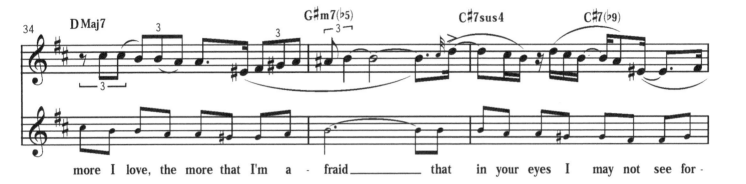

more I love, the more that I'm a - fraid_____ that in your eyes I may not see for-

e - ver,___ for - e - ver. If we can be the best of lov - ers

yet be the best of friends, If we can try with ev'-ry day to make it bet-ter as it

grows, with an - y luck then I sup - pose_____ the mu - sic ne - ver

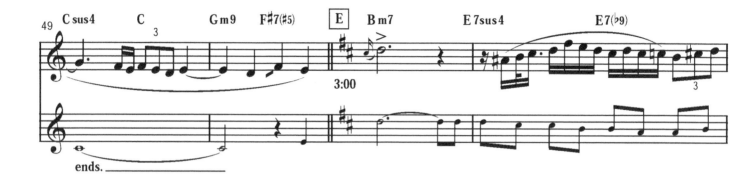

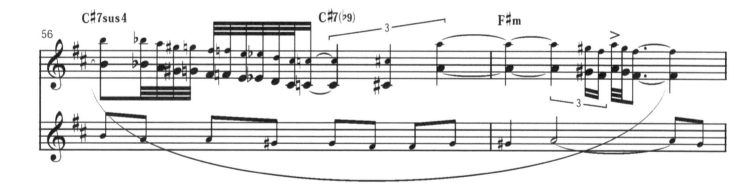

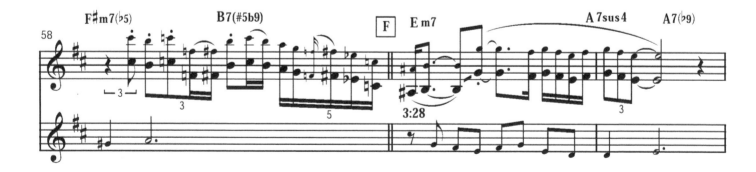

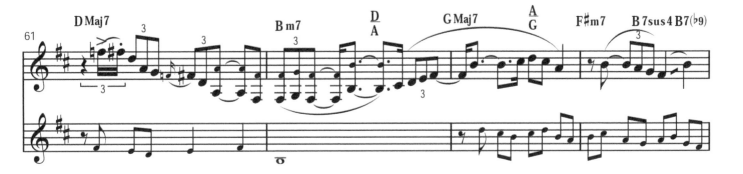

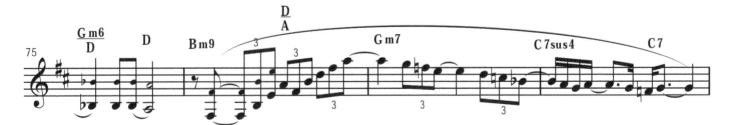

SOLO B♭ TRUMPET
(FLUGELHORN)

It's Only a Paper Moon

Words by BILLY ROSE and E.Y. HARBURG
Music by HAROLD ARLEN

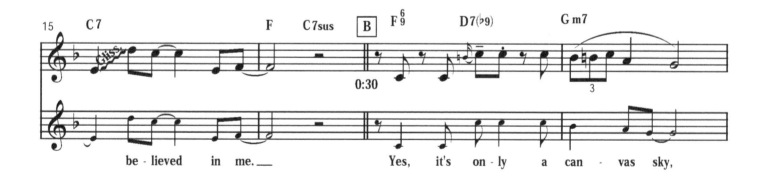

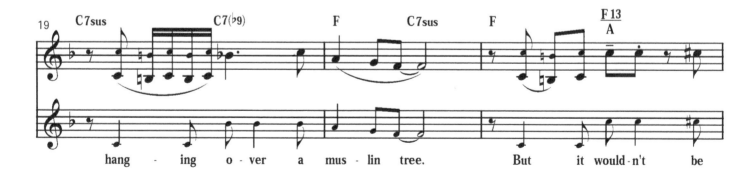

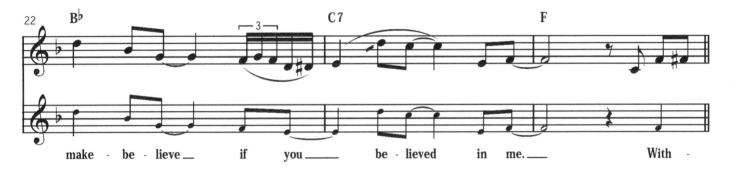

make - be - lieve ___ if you ___ be - lieved in me. ___ With -

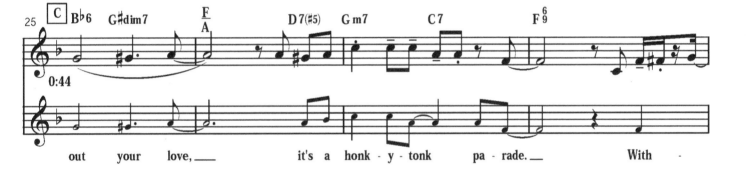

out your love, ___ it's a honk - y - tonk pa - rade. ___ With -

out your love, ___ it's a mel - o - dy played in a pen - ny ar - cade.

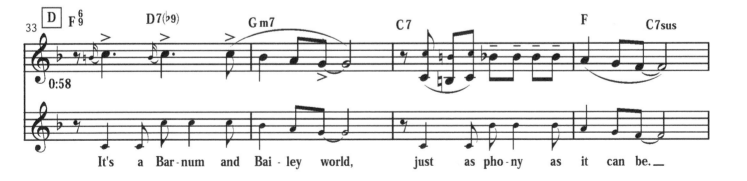

It's a Bar - num and Bai - ley world, just as pho - ny as it can be. ___

But it would-n't be make-be-lieve if you ___ be-lieved in me. ___

SOLO B♭ TRUMPET
(FLUGELHORN)

Samba de Orfeo
(Samba de Orphee)

Words by ANTONIO MARIA and ANDRE SALVET
Music by LUIZ BONFA

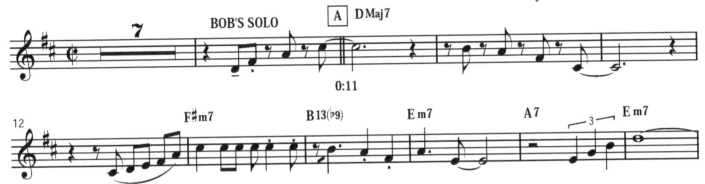

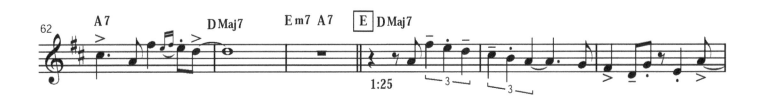

26

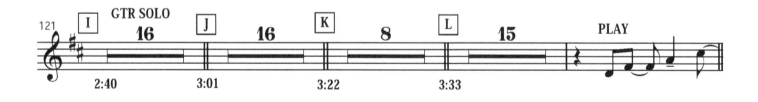

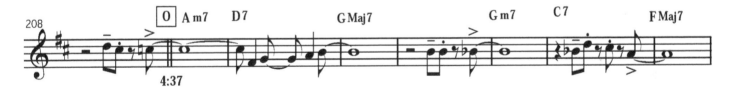

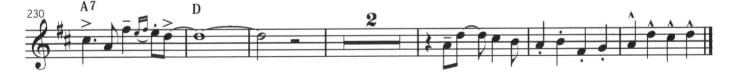

SOLO B♭ TRUMPET
(FLUGELHORN)

Blue Moon

Music by RICHARD RODGERS
Lyrics by LORENZ HART

MMO 6841

MMO 6841

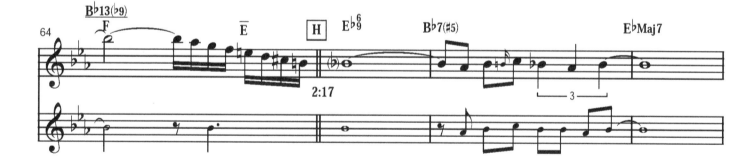

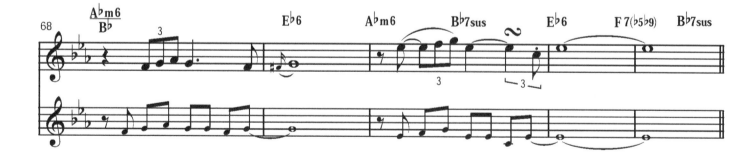

SOLO B♭ TRUMPET
(FLUGELHORN)

You Must Believe in Spring

Lyrics by ALAN and MARILYN BERGMAN
Music by MICHEL LEGRAND

When lone-ly feel-ings chill the mea-dows of your mind, just think if win-ter comes, can spring be far be-hind? Be-neath the deep-est snows, the se-cret of a rose is mere-ly that it knows you must be-lieve in spring. Just as a tree is sure it's leaves will re-ap-pear; It knows the emp-ti-ness is just the time of year.

You must be-lieve in love and trust it's on it's way, just as the sleep-ing rose a-

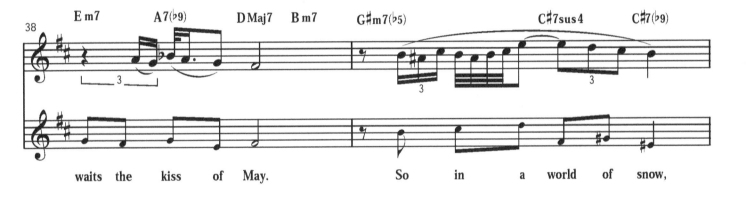

waits the kiss of May. So in a world of snow,

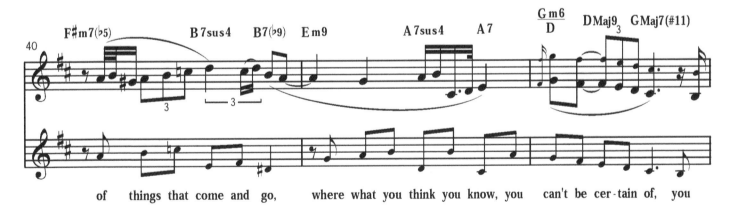

of things that come and go, where what you think you know, you can't be cer-tain of, you

must be-lieve in spring and love.

Black Orpheus

By LUIZ BONFA
and ANTONIO CARLOS JOBIM

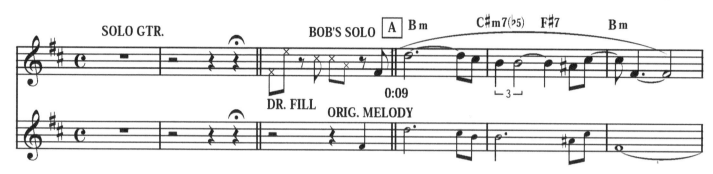

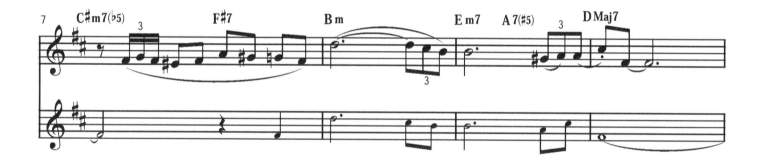

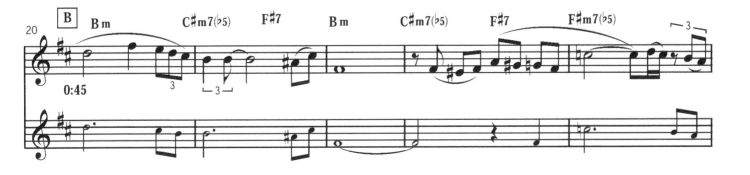

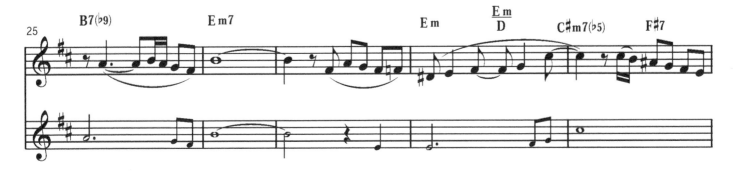

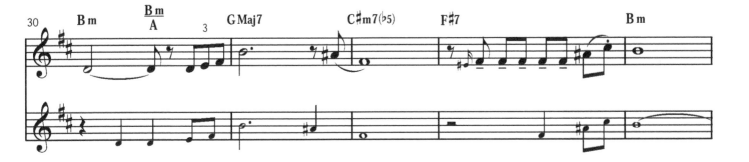

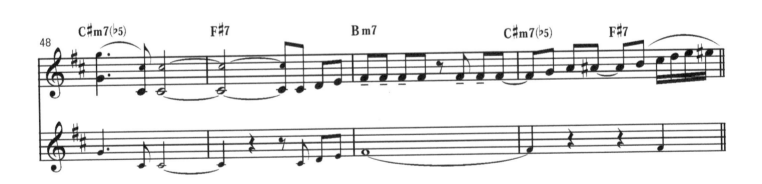

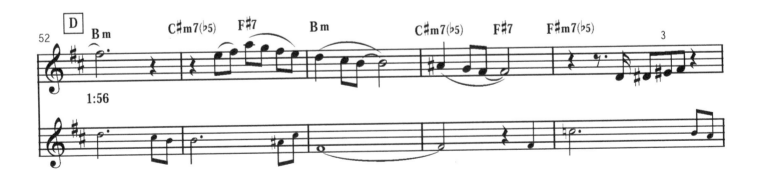

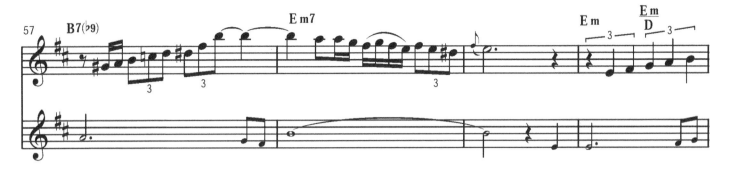

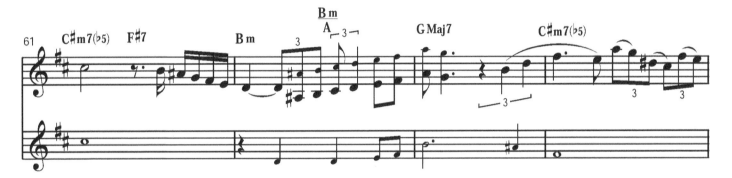

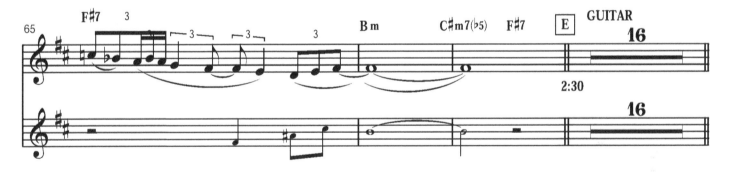

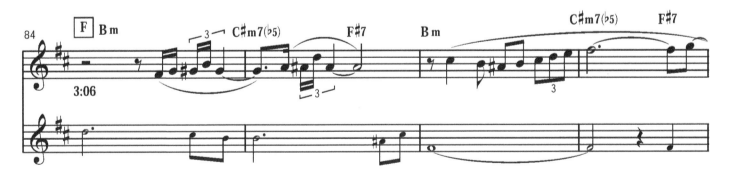

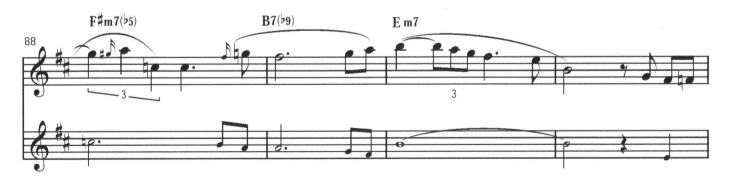

MMO 6841

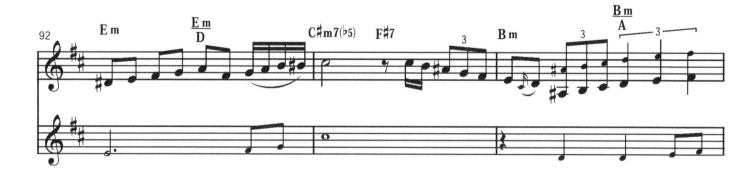

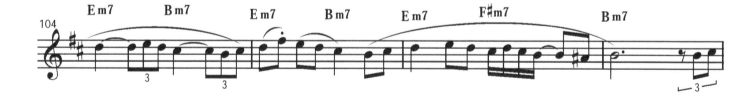

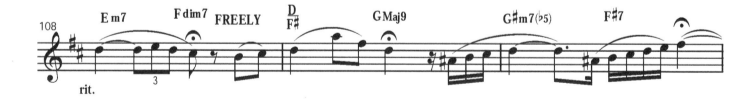

SOLO B♭ TRUMPET
(FLUGELHORN)

Fly Me to the Moon

Music and Lyrics by BART HOWARD

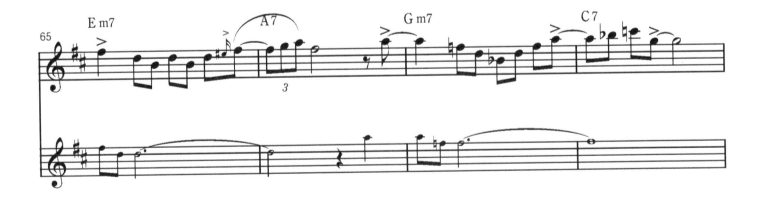

NOTES

I'VE BEEN ASKED THROUGHOUT MY CAREER as a performer and a teacher to put my ideas into a course or book with audio and perhaps at some point, I'll do just that. When I do, I promise you, it won't be the typical "How To Play Jazz" book that ends up on the bookshelf largely unread or unstudied! Until then, please consider this series of *Standards for Trumpet* a kind of mini-course that gives an overview of my approach to jazz improvisation.

When Irv Kratka, the founder of Music Minus One and Pocket Songs, asked me to write some notes and comments to accompany this first volume of **Standards for Trumpet**, my first thought was: How can I condense a lifetime of musical experiences into meaningful advice in just a few pages?

Aside from any other value these words may have, this was a fine opportunity to acknowledge the originator of the innovative "play-along" concept that eventually morphed into the hugely successful Karaoke. Is it a coincidence that I purchased the original Jazz MMOs as a teen back in the '50s and passed them down to my brother, Glenn, who literally devoured those masterful recordings that contained some of the finest jazz musicians of the time? And here am I, more than half a century later recording MMO audio to be enjoyed and hopefully put to practical use by you as we did with the first MMOs!

In making these recordings with various ensembles from big band to small Latin-based rhythm sections, I tried to find a balance between a musically satisfying performance and one that also has educational value in terms of providing some insight to what can be an elusive process, namely jazz improvisation.

From there, it was simply a matter of taking a standard song and playing it in a jazz style with enough liberty to transform it into a model or pattern for you to emulate. In this, what I'll call the foundational layer, I set out to be highly respectful of these wonderful melodies and only then add embellishments, excursions and challenges for you to confront, understand and integrate into your own playing.

An important point: Never be ashamed to imitate an artistic product of another that you admire. This has always been the time-honored way to acquire the ability to improvise. My own models are many and include classical composers such as Bach, Mozart and Bartok and the jazz greats Louis Armstrong, Charlie Parker, Miles Davis, Stan Getz, Bill Evans and Thelonious Monk.

I recommend you choose your models carefully, as you should with role models in other aspects of life, for they inevitably tend to influence you one way or another.

On to some brief comments on the ten songs of this Volume One in the series **Standards for Trumpet**:

Album numbers shown after each song represent the original arrangements we used to create the music for these recordings.

I chose **When You're Smiling** (PSCDG 6094) as the "opener" for its simplicity and history. I suggest you also listen to the classic versions by Louis Armstrong and the original Sinatra/Riddle recording to appreciate the potential of this simple song.

While we're here with Louis and Frank, two seemingly disparate artists, similarities do exist, especially the way they can so easily swing a melody. Granted Armstrong is generally considered to have almost invented jazz as we know it, and this is evident in the Hot Five and Seven recordings where he shone like a beacon. But even Miles Davis acknowledged Sinatra's unique phrasing.

So, the idea is to imagine standing in front of this hard-swinging band and just lay down the melody until it modulates up a half step to A Major concert, and this is the challenge part since we're rarely asked to improvise in five sharps, but truly there is very little technical difference from key to key other than familiarity. The sooner we accept that as logical, the more comfortable we'll be improvising. For example, consider the jazz standard *All the Things You Are* which goes through many keys!

In order to increase the intensity for the build-up to the end, I felt "invited" to jump into the upper octave, and then it was just a matter of riding the train to the end of the line with a climax and let the band cap it with a big, fat chord topped with a high F♯.

I'm in the Mood for Love (PSCDG 6195) is a lovely arrangement that was designed to highlight Streisand's singular vocal and expressive talent, and since the trumpet is also a soprano instrument as is Barbra's, it wasn't a quantum leap to step into her shoes. (Just a figure of speech, for I don't fancy myself in high heels!) The modulation from A♭ to B♭ (concert) is nice 'n' easy to navigate. The *rubato* ending is one that will take a few listenings to sync with the background smoothly.

Blue Bossa (MMO 3376) has an energetic Brazilian rhythm section over which to improvise. I chose to leave space and interact rather than fill every nook and cranny with notes which, in general, is my preference. As an overall tonal concept, remember the title is **BLUE Bossa**, which should happen without any particular effort because of the minor key and scale, diminished scales, flatted ninths, etc., which are all conducive to creating an overall bluesy sound.

How Do You Keep the Music Playing? (PSCDG 6195) is one of the many amazing songs composed by the great French musician Michel Legrand with lyrics by Alan and Marilyn Bergman. For us, the challenge at the start is to synch with the *rubato* accompaniment that was in Barbra Streisand's original arrangement. Now, we have to follow it!

I always study a song from as many angles as possible. Understanding the story, the ebb and flow, the building of intensity that reaches peaks, contrasted by the "valleys" of the song are essential in squeezing the most out of a performance!

Great singers like Billie Holiday, Ella Fitzgerald, Sinatra and Streisand are just some of the finest examples of masters and mistresses of the art of storytelling with song. And ultimately, you want to strive for this in your improvisations.

It's Only a Paper Moon (PSCDG 6094) is another spirited Sinatra/Riddle collaboration that you can plug into, in a key that I find to be one of the easiest to improvise in. *E♭ Major concert* lays so nicely for us because of the limited use of the third valve. Not that you should go into agreement with the so-called difficulty of one key over another, but more that it's kind of nice every so often to enjoy a "downhill" ride!

Samba de Orfeo (MMO 3376) is one of two classic songs by the great Brazilian composer Luiz Bonfa from the soundtrack of the movie *Black Orpheus* that allows us to float along with this unnecessary lively, authentic Brazilian rhythm section. Trading fours with them, which can be in some instances a challenge, shouldn't present any obstacles in the road to returning to the melody out section. Notice how nicely the piano player sets up the return to the out chorus.

Blue Moon (PSCDG 6094), usually a relaxed and romantic song, is now more of a hard-driving episode with this chart by Riddle that just invites you to stay close to the melody, as my "old boss" Frank Sinatra knew how to do so well, while putting his stamp of originality on it. A reminder: Never be afraid to state the melody. As you'll see in the transcriptions, slight rhythmical variations take it out of the realm of the dreaded (by many jazz musicians) straight melody.

You Must Believe in Spring (PSCDG 6175) is, as far as I'm concerned, ***the*** Legrand/Bergman masterpiece for many reasons! Aside from its exquisite melody and harmonic structure that defies a key center, it can be used as a major ear training tool. In fact, I'd venture to say that if you can sing this song in all twelve keys and play it on a given starting note from start to finish, you have made great strides towards being the jazz player of your dreams! I decided to use the flugelhorn on this pensive song for its rather haunting quality.

Black Orpheus (MMO 3376), or as it's known in English, *A Day in the Life of a Fool*, is the theme song from the cult classic film of the same name. I always find this lovely minor-key song an easy ride, in that unexplainable tradition that tempted Stan Getz in the 1960s and continues to weave its spell on us to this day. Just let the rhythm section lead you through the logical, almost predictable chord changes but, in some way, always inexplicably unique. Again, allowing space is a major part of the breath and breadth of this charming music called Bossa Nova that we've welcomed into the *Great American Song Book*.

Fly Me to the Moon (PSCDG 6096) is probably the stompinest (is that a word?) recording that Sinatra ever made, and I remember it well from those exciting years I spent in the trumpet section as part of what was called Frank's East Coast Band. The original recording was with the Basie Band playing this incredible chart by Quincy Jones. I visualized myself out in front of the band at the Sands in Vegas, in Frank's shoes, as it were, hopped on the train, plane or space shuttle, if you like, and let it *Fly Me to the Moon!*

When should you use the trumpet or the flugelhorn?

Back in the 1960s, it became a requirement for a professional, gigging trumpet player to own a flugelhorn and be able to switch at a couple of measures notice from one to the other. As part of his "arsenal," a busy player needed to have a piccolo trumpet and even a cornet.

Before then, it would be rare to see a flugel, as it was called for short, on jazz, big band and commercial gigs although it's not a 20th century invention. It stems back to its use in primarily the concert bands of the late 19th century, but it didn't become known by the general public until trumpeter Chuck Mangione switched to it and recorded his hit record *Feels So Good*. Miles Davis used its warm, dark tone in the 1950s to the fullest on the ground-breaking recordings and Carnegie Hall concert with Gil Evans. More and more trumpeters like Clark Terry, Art Farmer and others that leaned toward the mellow rather than fiery tone were found preferring it. I like to use it myself for contrast to the more strident timbre of the trumpet.

My flugelhorn is a three-valve French Quesnon, which is of classic design and light weight.

I've played a Bach trumpet most of my life with some very brief experiments with others. It's a Medium Large Bore, Light Weight Stradivarius with a 72 bell. My mouthpiece is a Zottola 64B Symphony Back Bore, which is equivalent to about a Bach 7D. I'm not much into experimenting with equipment these days but certainly have done my share in the past, especially because of having the luxury of my own personal mouthpiece maker, my father Frank, who was also my first teacher.

I've found now that by focusing primarily on the music that I hear in my mind, the rest, kind of, takes care of itself, in that I always sound like me, whatever equipment I use. The main thing is to play every day, even if only on the mouthpiece, although an occasional day off can be refreshing and even rejuvenating after a grueling gig. I remember hearing how Bud Herseth, principal trumpet in the Chicago Symphony, would just take his mouthpiece with him during summer vacation and keep in shape for his return to the "hot seat" in the orchestra!

I wish you great success in all your endeavors!

—*Bob Zottola*